Amazing Bees

FIRST EDITION
Series Editor Deborah Lock; **US Senior Editor** Shannon Beatty; **Editor** Arpita Nath;
Senior Art Editor Ann Cannings; **Art Editor** Yamini Panwar; **Producer, Pre-Production** Dragana Puvacic;
Picture Researcher Aditya Katyal; **DTP Designers** Syed Md Farhan, Dheeraj Singh;
Managing Editor Soma Chowdhury; **Managing Art Editor** Ahlawat Gunjan; **Art Director** Martin Wilson;
Reading Consultant Linda Gambrell, PhD

THIS EDITION
Editorial Management by Oriel Square
Produced for DK by WonderLab Group LLC
Jennifer Emmett, Erica Green, Kate Hale, *Founders*

Editors Grace Hill Smith, Libby Romero, Maya Myers, Michaela Weglinski;
Photography Editors Kelley Miller, Annette Kiesow, Nicole DiMella; **Managing Editor** Rachel Houghton;
Designers Project Design Company; **Researcher** Michelle Harris; **Copy Editor** Lori Merritt;
Indexer Connie Binder; **Proofreader** Larry Shea; **Reading Specialist** Dr. Jennifer Albro;
Curriculum Specialist Elaine Larson

Published in the United States by DK Publishing
1745 Broadway, 20th Floor, New York, NY 10019

Copyright © 2023 Dorling Kindersley Limited
DK, a Division of Penguin Random House LLC
23 24 25 26 10 9 8 7 6 5 4 3 2 1
001-334092-July/2023

All rights reserved.
Without limiting the rights under the copyright reserved above, no part of this publication may be reproduced, stored in or introduced into a retrieval system, or transmitted, in any form, or by any means (electronic, mechanical, photocopying, recording, or otherwise), without the prior written permission of the copyright owner.
Published in Great Britain by Dorling Kindersley Limited

A catalog record for this book
is available from the Library of Congress.
HC ISBN: 978-0-7440-7455-0
PB ISBN: 978-0-7440-7456-7

DK books are available at special discounts when purchased in bulk for sales promotions, premiums, fundraising, or educational use. For details, contact: DK Publishing Special Markets,
1745 Broadway, 20th Floor, New York, NY 10019
SpecialSales@dk.com

Printed and bound in China

The publisher would like to thank the following for their kind permission to reproduce their images:
a=above; c=center; b=below; l=left; r=right; t=top; b/g=background
Dreamstime.com: 2day929 17b, Pimmimemom 14bl, Sumikophoto 11cr, 16
Cover images: *Front:* **Dreamstime.com:** Daniel Prudek; *Spine:* **Dreamstime.com:** Anest

All other images © Dorling Kindersley
For more information see: www.dkimages.com

For the curious
www.dk.com

Level 2

Amazing Bees

Sue Unstead

Contents

6	Our Bee Friends
14	Bees and Flowers
20	Bee Families
26	Bee Spotting
30	Glossary
31	Index
32	Quiz

Our Bee Friends

Bees are amazing! They help flowers make fruits and seeds. They make sweet honey.

Let's find out why bees are so special.

What Is a Bee?

A bee is an insect. Like all insects, it has six legs. It has a body made up of three parts.

Buzz, buzz!

It has two pairs of wings.
A bee beats its wings
so fast it makes
a buzzing sound.

Close-Up View

Let's zoom in close.

A bee has a hairy body and face.

It has two big eyes and three little ones.

three little eyes

two big eyes

It has a very long tongue.

On its back legs, there are little baskets to collect pollen.

Sting Safe

A bee only stings if you disturb it, and only female bees have a stinger.

All these features help a bee do its jobs.

11

From Egg to Bee

A bee starts life as a tiny egg inside a wax cell. A white grub called a larva hatches from the egg. The bees usually feed the larva lots of pollen.

wax cell

It grows bigger and bigger in its cell. After many days, it becomes a pupa. The pupa changes slowly inside its cell. It comes out as an adult bee.

egg

larva

bee

Bees and Flowers

A bee is a flower's best friend. It helps the flower make seeds to make more flowers. It also helps the flower make the fruits and crops we eat.

The flower has food for the bees and larvae—sugary nectar and powdery pollen.

Sweet Nectar

A bee smells the flower and flies to it. It lands on a petal looking for the sweet, sugary juice.

Bee Vision

Sometimes flower petals have markings that only a bee can see. These are like signposts for bees—this way for a sweet treat!

The bee uncurls its long tongue and dips it deep inside the flower. Sip, sip, sip! It sucks up the nectar.

Sip!

Spreading Pollen

A bee may visit more than 50 flowers during one trip.

Bee Dancing

Honeybees dance to tell other bees where to find food. A "waggle dance," when a bee moves in a figure-eight shape, points bees in the direction of a nectar source.

The bee combs some of the pollen into the baskets on its back legs. Some of the pollen sticks to the bee's hairy body.

When the bee flies to other flowers, this pollen falls off. The pollen helps plants make fruit and seeds so that new plants grow.

Bee Families

One type of bee, the honeybee, lives in a big family group. Each bee has its own special job to do.

The biggest bee of all is the mother bee, called the queen. Her job is to lay eggs.

Bumblebees

Bumblebees live in family groups, too. They live in nests in the ground or in piles of dead leaves. Bumblebees are bigger and have more hair than honeybees. They make just a little honey and only enough for their hive.

Next in size are the drones, the male bees. The rest of the bees are females, called the worker bees.

Busy Bees

The worker bees are busy night and day. Some feed pollen to the baby bees, or larvae. Some look after the queen, feeding and grooming her. They make a special food called royal jelly for the queen.

Hives

Honeybees make wax called honeycomb that they use to build their homes, or hives. They can build their hives in a hollow tree, in a cave, or under a roof. The honeycomb is made up of wax cells. Each cell has six sides.

Other workers guard the nest, keep it clean, and build new cells. Many workers fly out of the hive to find nectar and pollen.

All About Honey

Honeybees make a sweet treat that we can eat: honey!

When a honeybee brings nectar to the nest, it passes the nectar to the mouth of another honeybee.

The nectar is passed from bee to bee. This turns it into honey.

The bees store the honey in wax cells that make up a honeycomb.

25

Bee Spotting

Not all bees live in big groups like the honeybee. Some bees live alone and build their own special nests.

A mound of soil on the grass could be the nest of a lawn bee.

A carpenter bee chews a hole in wood to make its nest.

A leafcutter bee makes neat round holes in leaves. It builds a nest like a tube out of leaves and cuts a circle for a lid.

Be a Friend to Bees

Bees are very important in helping plants make the food we eat. We can help bees by letting wildflowers grow or by planting flowers.

Then, watch the bees work as they fly from flower to flower!

Bees like flowers with lots of nectar and pollen. Here are some of them:

bluebell

clover

hollyhock

lavender

daisy

Enjoy, busy bees!

29

Glossary

Honey
Thick, sweet syrup made by bees

Honeycomb
Group of wax cells where honeybees live and store honey

Larva
Newly hatched wingless grub that will become an insect

Nectar
Sweet liquid found in flowers used to make honey

Pollen
Fine powder found on flowers

Pupa
Larva changing into an adult insect

Index

bumblebees 20

buzzing sound 9

carpenter bee 27

dance 18

drones 21

eggs 12, 13, 20

eyes 10

family groups 20–21

flowers 6, 14–19,
  28–29

hives 22, 23

honey 6, 24–25

honeybees 18, 20, 22,
  24–25

honeycomb 22, 25

insects 8

larva 12, 13, 15, 22

lawn bee 26

leafcutter bee 27

nectar 15, 16–17, 18,
  23, 25, 29

nest 23, 25, 26–27

pollen 11, 12, 15, 18–19,
  23, 29

pupa 13

queen bee 20, 22

stinger 11

tongue 11, 17

wax cell 12, 22, 25

wings 9

worker bees 21, 22–23

31

Quiz

Answer the questions to see what you have learned. Check your answers in the key below.

1. How many parts make up a bee's body?
2. Who is the biggest bee in a beehive?
3. Which is the only food made by insects that we can eat?
4. What sticks to a bee's body as it hunts for nectar?
5. What are female bees also called?

1. Three 2. Queen bee 3. Honey 4. Pollen 5. Worker bees